Williamson  Publishing

Make Your Own

HAIRWEAR

Beaded Barrettes, Clips, Dangles & Headbands

Diane Baker

Illustrations by

Alexandra Michaels

WILLIAMSON PUBLISHING • CHARLOTTE, VERMONT

Library of Congress Cataloging-in-Publication Data

Baker, Diane, 1951 July 9-
    Make your own hairwear : beaded barrettes, clips, dangles & headbands / Diane Baker ;
illustrations by ALexandra Michaels.
        p. cm. — (A Williamson quick starts for kids! book)
    Includes index.
    Summary: Provides step-by-step instructions for creating more than twenty beaded hair
accessories, including hair combs and clips, beaded bobby pins, headbands, etc.
    ISBN 1-885593-63-5 (pbk.)
    1. Beadwork—Juvenile literature. [1. Beadwork. 2. Handicraft.] I. Title: Hairwear. II.
Michaels, Alexandra, ill. III. Title. IV. Series.

TT860 .B325 2001
745.58'2—dc21

20010267701

Quick Starts for Kids!™ series editor: **Susan Williamson**
This material has been adapted from *Jazzy Jewelry* by Diane Baker.
Interior illustrations: **Alexandra Michaels**
Interior design: **Dana Pierson** and **Nancy-jo Funaro**
Cover design: **Marie Ferrante-Doyle**
Cover illustrations: **Michael Kline**
Cover photography: **Peter Coleman**
Printing: **Capital City Press**

Williamson Publishing Co.
P.O. Box 185
Charlotte, VT 05445
(800) 234-8791

Manufactured in the United States of America

10 9 8 7 6 5 4 3 2 1

Parts of this book have previously been published in *Jazzy Jewelry:
Power Beads, Crystals, Chokers, & Illusion and Tattoo Styles.*

Contents

Why Make Your Own Hairwear?   4

Jazzy Hair Holders   5

Beaded Tension Clips   6
Triple-Strand Tieback with Coil Bead   8
Beaded Tieback   10
Fringed Bobby Pin   11

"Beady" Creatures and Charms   15

Bobby Pin Trefoil   16
Flower & Pearl Hair Pin   18
Delicate Dragonfly   20
Beaded Bow Tie   23
Shining Star Charm   25
"Beady" Bumblebee Charm   30
Five-Petal Flower Garden   32
Lovely Ladybug Charm   34

Floating-on-Air Illusions   35

Butterfly Hair Dangle   37
Pearl & Seed Bead Illusion Headband   38
Swinging Hair Dangle   40
Crystal & Pearl Cluster Illusion Headband   42
Magic Hair Sparkler   43
Triple-Strand Illusion Headband   44
Stretchy Rhinestone Illusion Headband   46
Hair Snappers   48

Bold Barrettes and Clasps   49

Bugle Bead Barrette   50
Colorful Clay Clasp   51

Techniques   53

"Must-Have" Supplies   56

Index   63

Why Make Your Own Hairwear?

I'll bet you see great hair accessories in shops all the time. Much of it is good-looking and inexpensive. So why should you bother making your own?

 The #1 Reason: It's Fun!

Making hair trinkets can be as relaxing or as challenging as you want. With so many designs and styles to create and a world full of beautiful beads to collect, how could you ever be bored again?

 It Makes You Smarter!

It's true! While you're having fun making all these beautiful things to wear, you're exercising a big chunk of your mind! It takes brain power to visualize a piece of jewelry in your mind and then make it into something real. You're taking an idea from the "thinking about it" stage to the "creating it and finishing it" stage (a very handy skill)!

 It's Better (and Cheaper)

The reason hairwear in stores is sometimes inexpensive is because the manufacturers aren't using high-quality materials or crafting skills. They use plastic beads instead of glass, for example. Or, they may offer only one or two colors. Making your own usually means spending less and ending up with a better-quality piece.

 You Can Have It *Your* Way

When you make your own accessories, you can have exactly what you like: the exact style, the exact color, the exact length. You can re-create what you've admired in the store (or on a friend!), or you can experiment with your own ideas (hey, you just might start a hot new style!).

 You'll Get Better Acquainted with an Awesome Person — You!

As you create something yourself, you'll make decisions large (Which hair accessory goes best with your outfit?) and small (Which accent bead looks best at the end of this strand?). Each one teaches you a little more about your likes and dislikes.

So, ready to get started?

If you've done any beading or craft projects at home in the past, you may already have the materials you need to jump right into some of the easier designs. To make sure you're well stocked, check out pages 56–62 for a list of the basic beading supplies and handy tools needed for all the hairwear in this book.

Jazzy Hair Holders

A simple strand full of beads – the easiest beading technique – can transform plain clips, tiebacks, or pins lying all over the top of your bureau into pieces of jewelry. All it takes is a length of wire or thread and beads in your favorite styles and colors, and before you know it, you'll have a jazzy collection of hair ornaments!

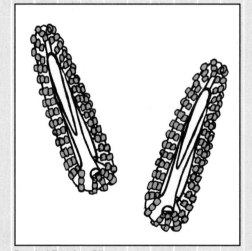

Beaded Tension Clips

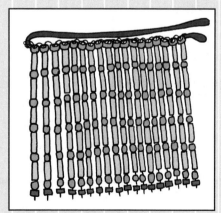

Fringed Bobby Pin

Beaded Tension Clips

A few seed beads can jazz up an ordinary hair clip in no time and put some sparkle in your hair! Seed beads come in a rainbow of colors, so make a pair to match every outfit.

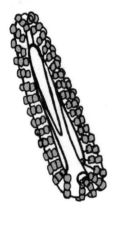

How difficult?
Moderate

Time:
45 minutes

What you need

Tension hair clip (1 pair)

36" (90 cm) of 34-gauge beading wire

Seed beads (about 120), in the color of your choice

Scissors, nail clippers, or wire cutters

1 Push one end of the beading wire through the small hole at the bottom of the tension clip and wrap it around the clip three or four times. Tuck the end under the wrapped section to secure it.

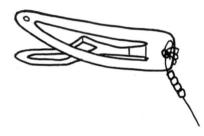

2 Slide on enough beads to cover the width of the clip.

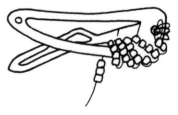

3 Wrap the beaded section around the clip, bringing the wire up the other side. Continue adding beads and wrapping the wire until you've covered the entire clip and are back at the hole.

4 Push the wire through the hole and secure it, as you did in step 1. Snip off the excess wire.

stretch
your creative muscles!

- **A Touch of Elegance.** Wire a crystal bead or a freshwater pearl to the clip.

- **Yipes! Stripes!** Try varying bead colors to make stripes. Or, alternate four or five shades of the same color seed bead to create a shimmery effect.

Quick Starts Tips!™

While You're Beading ...

Instead of keeping your beads on the table top, where they might roll off and get lost in the carpet, pour your beads onto white paper plates or into yogurt lids or shallow bowls. You'll be able to see all the colors, and the beads will be easy to get at.

TRY, TRY AGAIN.

Don't worry if it takes a couple of times before your work looks like something you want to wear. Your first try won't look as good as your second, and your second won't look as good as your third. Just take out your scissors, cut up your work, recycle the beads, and start again.

If you're like most people, you're going to make mistakes. Each time I make a mistake, I feel relieved because I've gotten that mistake over with and I won't have to do it again! (Probably. At least, I hope.) Now there's one less mistake in my future!

Triple-Strand Tieback with Coil Bead

Coil beads are actually tightly wound coils of brightly colored metal wire. They come in all kinds of interesting shapes and colors. With their large holes, they're a fun way to join multi-strands for a look that's quite different from the usual scrunchie or colored elastic.

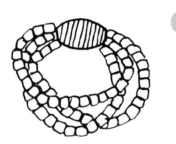

How difficult?
Easy!

Time:
45 minutes

What you need

12" (30 cm) of elastic thread

Tape

Beading needle

Coil bead

Seed beads (approximately 120)

Scissors

1 Secure one end of the thread with a piece of tape; thread the other end through the needle. String on the coil bead, pulling it about two-thirds of the way down the strand. Add as many seed beads as it takes to fit a ponytail snugly.

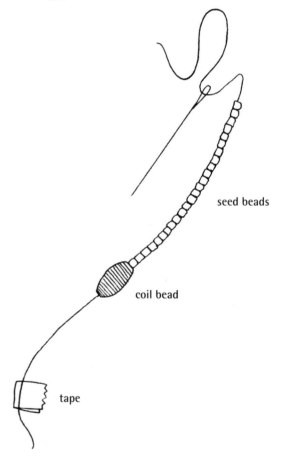

seed beads

coil bead

tape

2 Bring the needle through the coil bead again, forming the first strand.

3 String the same number of seed beads and bring the needle through the coil bead to form the second strand.

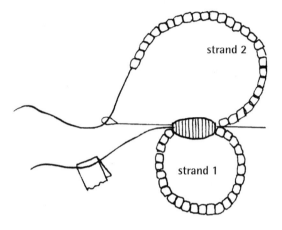

strand 2

strand 1

4 String on half the number of beads and secure them with tape.

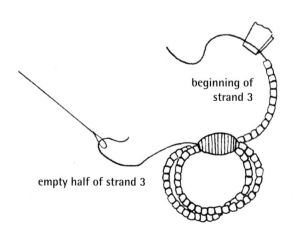

beginning of strand 3

empty half of strand 3

5 Remove the tape on the other thread; thread the needle onto it. String on the remaining beads.

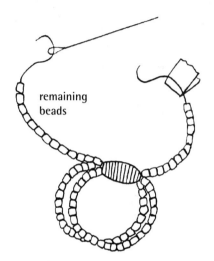

remaining beads

6 Tie the ends together with a lock knot*. Trim the threads.

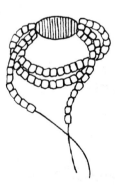

*See Techniques, pages 53–55.

Beaded Tieback

Can an elastic hair tieback be a fashion accessory? Sure – when you decorate it with your favorite beads! Use a mixture, including a few tiny teardrops or semiprecious stone chips for color.

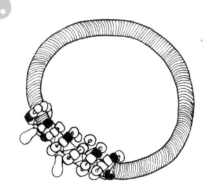

How difficult?
Easy!

Time:
20 minutes

What you need

18" (45 cm) of 34-gauge beading wire

Elastic hair tieback

Seed beads (about 50), in a mix of colors

Small accent beads (3 to 4)

Scissors, nail clippers, or wire cutters

1 Twist one end of the wire around the tieback several times near the metal crimp, bringing it under the prior loops to secure it.

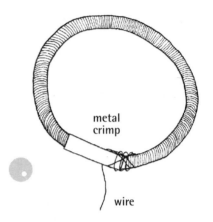

metal crimp

wire

2 Slide the beads onto the wire, interspersing the accent beads along the strand. Now, wrap the wire around the hair tieback, covering the metal crimp.

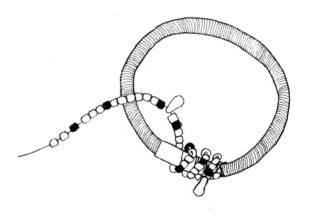

3 Wrap the end of the wire around the tieback several times; then, pull the end through the loops to secure it. Snip off the excess wire.

Fringed Bobby Pin

This fringe falls at whatever angle the bobby pin rests in your hair, so use it to pull back your bangs or to hold the wisps around your ponytail or braid.

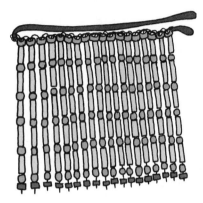

How difficult? Moderate to challenging

Time: 1 hour (faster with practice)

What you need

18" (45 cm) of 34-gauge beading wire

Bobby pin

Chopstick or pencil

Size 11 green iridescent seed beads (about 96)

Beading needle

Scissors, nail clippers, or wire cutters

24" (60 cm) of beading thread

Crimps (about 16)

Needle-nose pliers

Silver bugle beads (about 90)

Glue

To bead the bobby pin:

1 Wrap one end of the 18" (45 cm) section of beading wire around one end of the bobby pin so the wire is firmly attached.

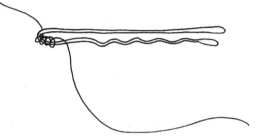

2 Wedge the pin open with the chopstick or pencil to hold it while you work. Slide on one seed bead and wrap the wire around the pin.

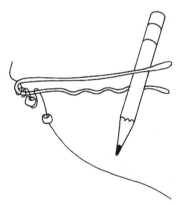

Continue wrapping and beading until you've covered the top of the pin.

3 Wrap the wire around the pin several times and pull it through the coil to be sure everything is nice and tight. Trim the ends.

To make the fringe:

4 Thread the needle with the 24" (60 cm) piece of beading thread; attach a crimp* to the other end.

5 Using the crimp method as shown on the next page, add beads in this pattern to make two fringes at a time:

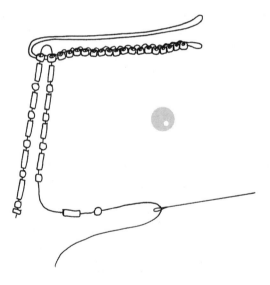

Add a drop of glue to the crimp at the bottom of each fringe and let dry.

6 Repeat steps 4 and 5 until you have filled the pin with fringe.

The Savvy Bead Buyer

BUGLE BEADS: Perfect for Fringes!

Long, slender **bugle beads** add just the right "shimmy" to your fringe. They come in sizes up to 2" to 3" (5 to 7.5 cm) long. Some even twist into wonderful spirals or are **faceted** (cut on an angle) so they reflect the light as they swing.

*See Techniques, pages 53–55.

HOW-TO

Make fringe with crimps:

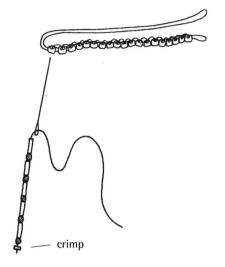

— crimp

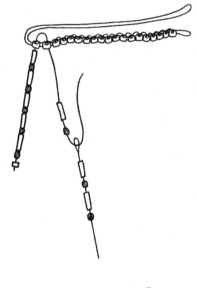

— crimp

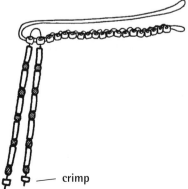

— crimp

Lightweight fringe. For an airier fringe, skip two beads between each fringe.

Symmetrical fringe. String a pattern of varying lengths.

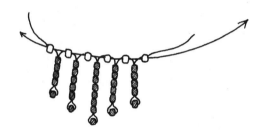

Decorated fringe. Try crystals, hearts, stars, or semiprecious chips at the bottom of each strand for a unique look.

HOMEMADE BUGLE BEADS

In addition to using store-bought bugle beads, why not use paper to make great, multi-colored bugle beads in sizes and shapes you want. Begin by cutting paper into very long, thin strips. Experiment with lots of different lengths and widths for different bead shapes. You'll end up with some very attractive beads!

What you need

Brightly colored paper (magazine pages, origami paper, wrapping paper, etc.)

Ruler, pencil, scissors, glue

Long, thin objects such as paintbrushes, pencils, toothpicks, skewers, etc.

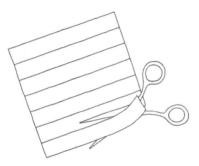

Cut 1" (2.5 cm) strips.

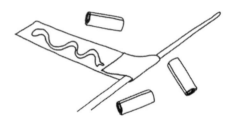

Roll paper strip on long, thin object (the thinner the object, the thinner your bead) and glue.

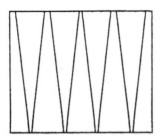

Try cutting your strips in long, thin triangles to see what kind of beads you come up with!

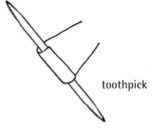

toothpick

Try using different items as rollers. You'll end up with different widths and thicknesses.

"Beady" Creatures and Charms

Dragonflies, ladybugs, flowers, stars, tiny bows — here are all your favorite beaded creatures and shapes to sparkle as you step! To make these "beadies," you simply shape a beaded strand of wire or use the easy "double-weave" technique (remember the Beady Buddy craze?). Then, wire them onto your bobby pins, clips, combs, or headbands and wear them whenever you want some color and flash!

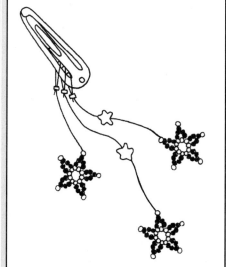

Star Dangler

Delicate Dragonfly

Bobby Pin Trefoil

You can bead bobby pins in a half-dozen ways. This combines the easiest with an elegant trefoil (three petal) design garnished with a glowing crystal.

How difficult?
Easy!

Time:
30 minutes

What you need

18" (45 cm) of 34-gauge beading wire

Bobby pin

Chopstick or pencil

Seed beads (34) for the bobby pin, in the color of your choice

Scissors, nail clippers, or wire cutters

Seed beads (63) for the trefoil, in the color of your choice

12" (30 cm) of 34-gauge beading wire

6-mm crystal

To bead the bobby pin:

1 Wrap one end of the 18" (45 cm) section of beading wire around one end of the bobby pin so it's firmly attached.

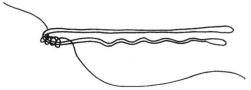

2 Wedge the pin open with the chopstick or pencil to hold it while you work. Slide on one seed bead and wrap the wire around the pin. Continue wrapping and beading until you've covered the top of the pin.

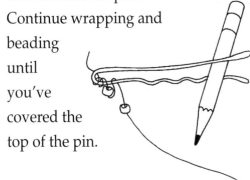

3 Wrap the wire around the pin several times and pull it through the coil to be sure everything is nice and tight. Trim the ends.

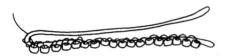

To make the trefoil:

4 Slide 21 beads onto the center of the 12" (30 cm) of 34-gauge beading wire. Bend this section into a petal shape. Holding the bottom of the petal shape, twist the petal to secure the loop.

5 Repeat on one side, then the other, to form your trefoil.

6 Slide your crystal onto one end of the wire.

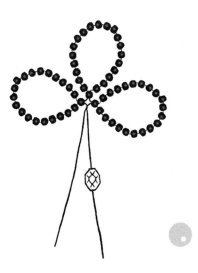

Bend the wire so that the crystal covers the twisted bases of the petal shapes. Move the shapes until you get a look you like. Use the remaining wire to fasten your trefoil onto the end of the bobby pin. Tuck the ends in and clip them closely.

Flower & Pearl Hair Pin

The pin disappears in your hair, leaving this flower magically "floating."

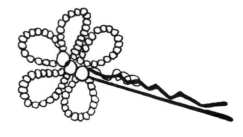

How difficult?
Easy!

Time:
30 minutes

What you need

Seed beads (100), in the color of your choice

10" (25 cm) of 22- or 24-gauge beading wire

3-mm pretend pearls (3)

Bobby pin

1 Slide 20 beads onto the wire. Bend the beaded section into a petal shape and twist the base to secure it.

2 Repeat, adding 20 beads each time, to form four more petals. Spread them out into a flower shape.

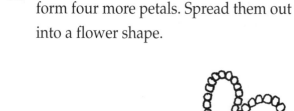
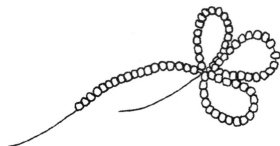

3 Bring one end of the wire up between two petals and slide on the three pearls. Center them on the flower so that they conceal the twisted bases.

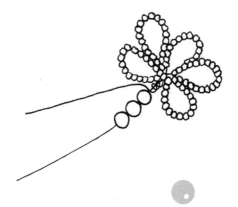

4 Bend both wire ends around to the back of the flower and use them to fasten the flower onto a bobby pin.

Want a Larger Flower? If you've got thick or very curly hair, try a bigger, more dramatic flower. Use a 12" (30 cm) length of wire, about 140 seed beads, and either a 7-mm crystal of a contrasting color or one pretend pearl as a finishing touch. Wire the flower to a larger bobby pin or a hair comb.

Quick Starts Tips!™

Hair Combs

Hair combs are, without a doubt, the most versatile hair ornament. Inexpensive plastic combs come four or six to a pack, so share a package among friends. Use them to smooth the sides of a ponytail, to hold a side part, to sweep back hair to show off your earrings, or to decorate a French twist. Of course, you'll want to embellish them with beadies first!

Delicate Dragonfly

This airy dragonfly alights on a bobby pin, comb, headband, or clip. Silver-lined beads and shiny black-green seed beads are perfect for creating a dragonfly's natural iridescent flash.

How difficult?
Moderate

Time:
1 hour

What you need

Black-green opalescent seed beads (48)

15" (37.5 cm) of 22- or 24-gauge beading wire

4-mm black bead

Silver-lined blue seed beads (104)

5-mm pale blue crystal

Needle-nose pliers

Scissors, nail clippers, or wire cutters

To form the body:

1 Slide 32 of the black-green seed beads onto the wire. Fold the wire in half so there are 16 beads on each side.

Twist it gently three times so it looks like this:

2 Holding the wires together, slip on the large black bead.

SPECIAL FINISHES!

Seed beads come in an amazing range of finishes for wonderful special effects. **Iridescent** beads shimmer with a prism effect, pearly **opalescent** beads quietly glow, and **silver-lined** beads (yes, the hole walls are silver-toned) gleam because light reflects through the glass. These beads may be a little more expensive, but they are well worth it.

The Savvy Bead Buyer

To form the lower wings:

3 Spread the unbeaded wires out to each side. Slide 20 blue seed beads onto one wire, form a loop, and twist the wing to "lock" it. Repeat on the other side.

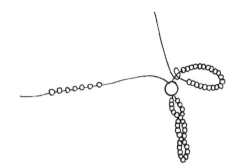

To form the upper wings:

4 Move the right wire to the left side and the left wire to the right side.

Add 32 blue beads to one wire, form a loop, and twist the wing to "lock" it. Repeat on the other side.

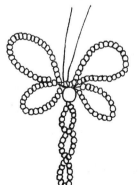

To form the head:

5 Slide three black-green beads onto each wire to make the neck. Then, holding the wires together, slide on the blue crystal for the head. Slide five black-green beads onto each wire to form antennae.

Kink* the ends; then snip off the excess wire.

To attach your "beady" to a bobby pin, comb, headband, or clip, follow the directions on page 22.

*See Techniques, pages 53–55.

ATTACHING YOUR "BEADIES"

You'll never run out of places to show off your "beadies!" They're perfect for decorating hair accessories like pins, combs, and even plastic headbands.

If you want your "beady" firmly attached:

Wire it on using narrow (34-gauge) beading wire. Then, bring the remaining wire under your loops to secure. Snip off the excess wire.

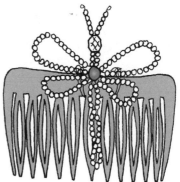

If you want your "beady" to dangle:

Simply wire it on a jump ring available at any bead or craft store.

Beaded Bow Tie

Once you get the hang of these tiny charming bows, you'll be able to whip up a pair in minutes. They're so cute that you'll want to use them in lots of ways (in addition to adorning your hair!).

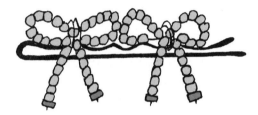

How difficult?
Moderate

Time:
10 minutes per bow tie (faster with practice)

What you need

10" (25 cm) of beading thread (2)

Tape

Beading needle

Seed beads (66), in the color of your choice

Crimps (4)

Needle-nose pliers

Scissors, nail clippers, or wire cutters

Glue

To make each bow tie:

1 Secure one end of the thread with a piece of tape; thread the other end through the needle. String 17 seed beads and slide them onto the middle of the thread.

Draw the needle back through the seventh bead you strung on (now called the "middle bead") from the direction shown.

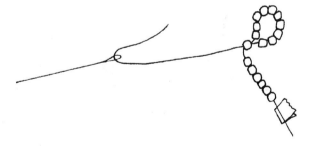

You just formed a beaded loop and the first bow "tail."

2 String 10 more beads. Make another loop, passing through the same middle bead again as shown. String six beads.

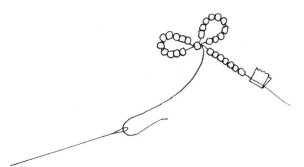

3 Attach a crimp* just below the beads on each "tail." Trim the threads below the crimps. Add a drop of glue on each end to be sure the thread doesn't pull out.

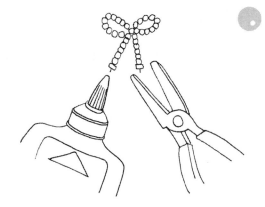

After the glue is dry, fiddle with the bow tie until the shape hangs nicely.

*See Techniques, pages 53–55.

stretch your creative muscles!

- **Transform Your Tanks and Ts.** Decorate the scoop necklines of your favorite summer shirts with these tiny bows. Just sew on a couple of beads in the loop and let the ends dangle.

To attach the bow to a bobby pin, comb, headband, or clip, follow the directions on page 22.

Shining Star Charm

With just a little practice, you can turn out a whole constellation of these tiny stars in under an hour.

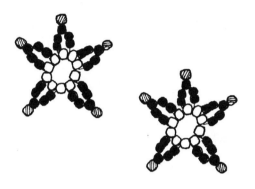

How difficult?
Moderate

Time:
15 minutes

What you need

12" (30 cm) of beading thread

Tape

Beading needle

Size 11 gold beads (10)

Size 11 deep blue beads (25)

Size 11 silver beads (5)

Scissors

To form the center of the star:

1 Secure one end of the thread with a piece of tape; thread the other end through the needle. String the gold beads. Pull the needle and thread through the first bead you strung on, forming a loop.

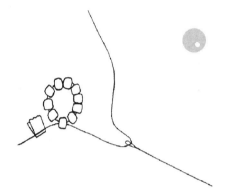

Tie the thread to the loop with a lock knot*.

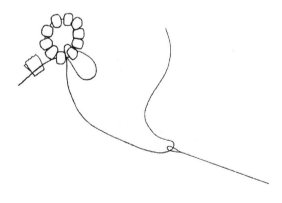

*See Techniques, pages 53–55.

To form each star point:

2 Follow these two steps:

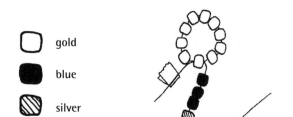

☐ gold

■ blue

▨ silver

3 Repeat step 2 four more times until you've come back around to the lock knot and formed a five-pointed star.

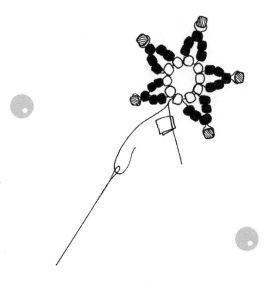

To finish:

4 Tie the thread with a lock knot and trim it.

Skip a gold bead and go through the next one

String on two more blue beads

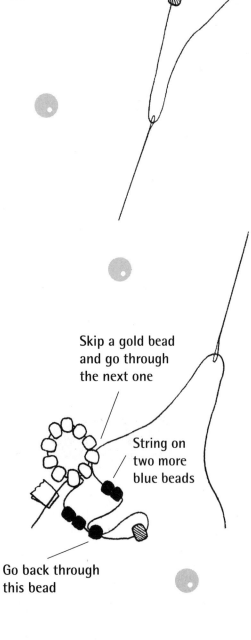

Go back through this bead

To attach your star to a bobby pin, comb, headband, or clip, follow the directions on page 22.

Starry, Starry Night. How about a sprinkle of silvery or pearl stars along the scoop neckline of a black T-shirt? It takes only minutes to stitch them on!

Stars A-Dangling. How about dangling star charms at the end of a Swinging Hair Dangle (see page 40) for the effect of glittering stars throughout your hair!

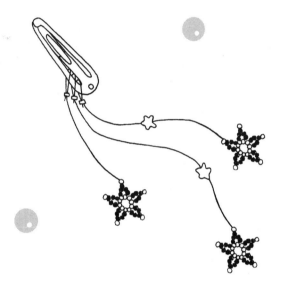

Quick Starts Tips!™

Passing Through Twice ...

Anytime you need to pass through a seed bead twice, check the hole to be sure it's nice and even, so the double thickness of thread can fit through easily.

DO THE DOUBLE WEAVE!

It'll take you only a minute or two to get the hang of this useful beading technique. Let's say you're going to double-weave a strip that is four beads wide:

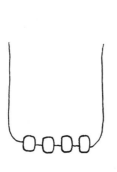

1. Slide on four beads.

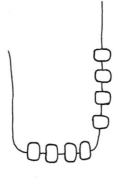

2. Slide on another four beads.

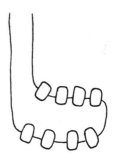

3. Bring this first row parallel to the bottom row.

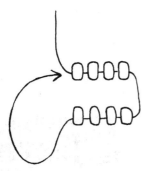

4. Push this wire through the top row in the opposite direction.

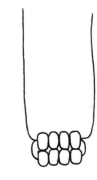

5. Pull this wire tight. Then, repeat steps 2 to 5 until you have the length you want.

Double-Weaving, continued

Illustrations for double-weave patterns typically look like this one. It shows you how many beads and what color to use for each row.

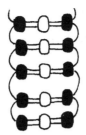

The finished "beady" will look like this.

To finish the ends:

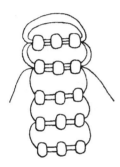

Weave the wires back through the last two rows.

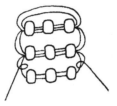

Wrap them around the wires on the edges.

Trim them and tuck in the ends.

Quick Starts Tips!™

Seed Bead Tips

Misshapen seed beads will give a lumpy, uneven result to your weaving, so pick through your beads to be sure you choose ones with a uniform size and shape. If size 11 seed beads are too difficult for you to handle comfortably, try a larger size, such as 8 or 6 (the higher the number, the smaller the bead).

"Beady" Bumblebee Charm

Double-weave a tiny striped bee! The iridescent beads (see page 20) give it just the right sparkle and flash.

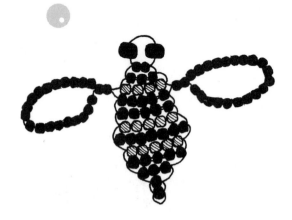

How difficult?
Moderate

Time:
30 minutes

What you need

24" (60 cm) of 34-gauge beading or brass wire

Size 6 black beads (2)

Iridescent black seed beads (74)

Bright yellow seed beads (14)

Scissors, nail clippers, or wire cutters

To form the head:

1 Make a loop with the wire. Slide one size 6 black bead onto each end of the wire. Slide two black seed beads onto one wire and double-weave (see Do the Double Weave!, page 28) them.

To start the body:

2 Double-weave the seed beads as shown.

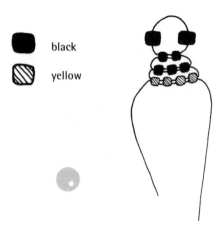

- ■ black
- ▨ yellow

To form the wings:

3 Slide 21 black seed beads onto one wire. Push the wire back through the first two seed beads as shown to form a loop.

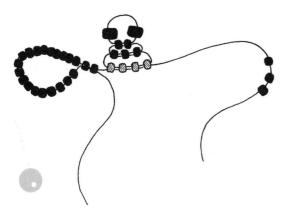

Repeat on the other side.

To finish the body and make the stinger:

4 Double-weave the seed beads in this pattern.

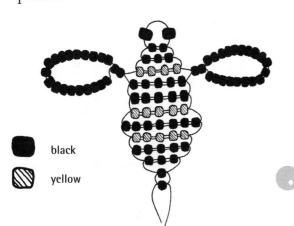

- ■ black
- ▨ yellow

5 To finish the ends, see page 29.

To attach your "beady" to a bobby pin, comb, headband, or clip, follow the directions on page 22.

Quick Starts Tips!™

If You Love It, Buy It!

New beads come into the craft and bead stores all the time, and space is limited, so if you see something you absolutely love, especially an unusual charm or accent bead, grab it because it may not be there the next time you come in. Don't worry if you don't know exactly how you'll use it. Beads don't go stale, they don't go out of style, and you don't have to worry about outgrowing them!

Five-Petal Flower Garden

This lovely row of posies uses the same technique as the Beaded Bow Tie (see page 23) to form five loops. Just as you are wondering how the petals are going to come together, suddenly, with one little twist, it's a flower!

How difficult?
Moderate

Time:
45 minutes

What you need

Seed beads for the flower (50), in the color of your choice

12" (30 cm) of 34-gauge beading wire

4- or 5-mm crystal or other accent bead

Scissors, nail clippers, or wire cutters

1 Slide on 11 beads about three-fourths of the way down the wire. Push one end of the wire through the first bead you strung on (now called the "middle bead") as shown to make the first petal's loop.

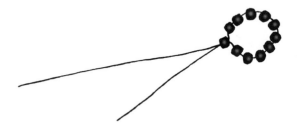

2 On the longer side of the wire, slide on 11 more beads and make another loop by passing through a new "middle bead" as described in step 1.

Repeat this step until you have a total of five petals.

3 Twist the two ends of the wire together to close the petals into a circle, forming a flower.

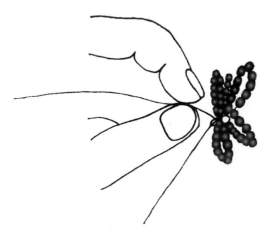

4 Slide the crystal bead onto the longer wire. To position the crystal in the center of the flower, bring that wire up between two petals and then down between two petals on the other side. Now, slide the shorter wire through the crystal.

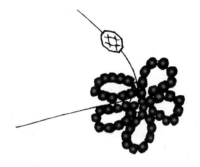

Quick Starts Tips!™

Petals for Pennies!

Using wire instead of thread creates a flower that will hold its perfectly shaped petals. (Beading thread will stretch and loosen over time, causing the petals to droop.) Readily available at the hardware store for only pennies a foot, brass wire is more flexible than beading wire. You'll find it easier to work with, especially when you're new to double weaving (see pages 28–29).

To attach the flower to a bobby pin, comb, headband, or clip, follow the directions on page 22.

stretch
your creative muscles!

● **Rainbow Petals.** To create an accent of color in each petal, use a different color bead to start each string of 11 beads. Or create flowers in different colors and attach a row of them to a large bobby pin or thin plastic headband.

Lovely Ladybug Charm

Create a lovely ladybug – the bug that's all the rage – to rest on your hair or dangle from a bobby pin.

How difficult?
Moderate

Time:
30 minutes

What you need

18" (45 cm) of 34-gauge beading or brass wire

Size 11 black seed beads (about 20)

Size 11 red seed beads (about 50)

Scissors, nail clippers, or wire cutters

To attach the ladybug to a bobby pin, comb, headband, or clip, follow the directions on page 22.

1 Slide on three black beads for the first row and then four black seed beads for the second row.

Double-weave (see page 28) these two rows to secure the beginning of the charm. Then, double-weave the ladybug shown here:

 black

 red

2 To finish, weave the remaining wires back through the last two rows (see page 29).

your creative muscles!

More "Beady" Magic. How about a matching pair of earrings? Just add jump rings to your beady charms and then dangle them wherever you like!

Floating-on-Air Illusions

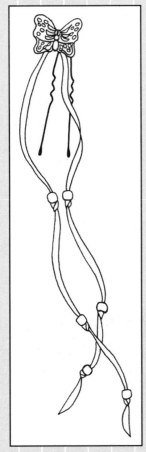

Butterfly Hair Dangle

The magic of illusion accessories is the way the beads and charms appear to float on or lie scattered in your hair. The trick is to use a special clear stringing material. You can create all the popular hair accessories (plus create your own style!) by varying the number of strands, spacing beads evenly or scattering them irregularly, and suspending one or more charms.

Triple-Strand Illusion Headband

THE ILLUSION TECHNIQUE

To create the effect that your beads are "floating," you string them on *monofilament* (also sold as illusion cord), which comes in a fantastic stretchy version, too. Stretchy monofilament is the most expensive of all the strand materials, but this stuff is so fun and easy to work with (just crimp the ends together and you're finished!), plus it lies flat and won't kink. You'll find two weights: thick and thin. The regular (nonstretchy) beading monofilament (sold by weight) also costs a bit more, but it's quality stuff, too.

Quick Starts Tips!™

Can't Find Monofilament?

You can also use fishing line from a hardware or sporting goods store, and a few dollars' worth will stretch to the moon and back. Check it out — you'll get hooked!

Butterfly Hair Dangle

A hair pin works perfectly to give the illusion of an elegant gold butterfly alighting on your head. Let the ribbons sway with your hair or dangle them from your ponytail, French braid, or twist for a sophisticated look.

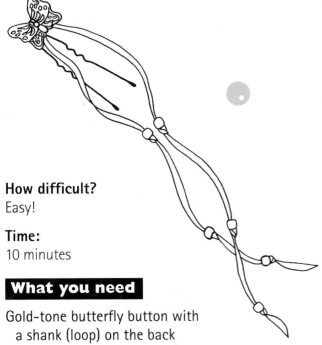

How difficult?
Easy!

Time:
10 minutes

What you need

Gold-tone butterfly button with a shank (loop) on the back

Hair pin (from drugstore or beauty supply store)

Large crimps (2)

Needle-nose pliers

22" (55 cm) of narrow gold fabric ribbon

4-mm beads (6), in clear, gold, or a color to match your outfit

1 Slide the butterfly button onto the center of the pin; attach a crimp* on both sides.

2 Center the ribbon on the shank and tie it on with a double knot*.

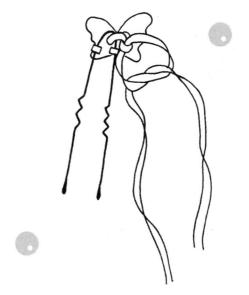

3 Decorate each side of the ribbon with beads as shown in the finished dangler, securing each one with a single knot*.

*See Techniques, pages 53–55.

Pearl & Seed Bead Illusion Headband

You can have a real pearl head-band for well under $5 using 5-mm *freshwater*, also called *natural*, pearls (see page 39). The *opalescent* seed beads (see page 20) offset the natural luster and charming individual shapes of the pearls.

How difficult?
Moderate

Time:
45 minutes

What you need

Pencil

Piece of foam board or paper

Ruler or measuring tape

16" (40 cm) of thin stretchy clear monofilament

Tape

Beading needle

Black opalescent seed beads (7)

5-mm rose-toned freshwater pearls (7)

Crimp

Needle-nose pliers

Scissors

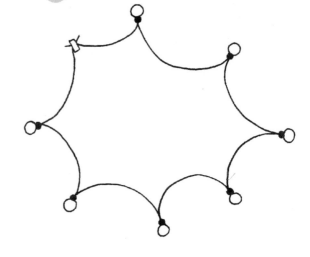

1 Draw a 2" (5 cm) line on the foam board or paper.

2 Secure one end of the monofilament with a piece of tape; thread the other end through the needle. String one seed bead and one pearl onto the strand and gently work them along to the center. Now, pull the monofilament back through the bottom of the seed bead so it sits on top of the pearl.

3 Using your line as a reference, string on the remaining six bead pairs following this pattern:

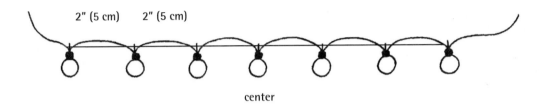

2" (5 cm)   2" (5 cm)

center

4 Hold the ends of the strand together and slip on the crimp. Holding the headband around your head, look in the mirror to adjust the length of the band to your own taste. Then, holding the ends at that length, attach the crimp*. Trim the ends of the monofilament if necessary.

The Savvy Bead Buyer

BUYING PEARLS

If you love the look of pearls, you can go wild with the plastic ones, also called **pretend** or **faux** (foe) pearls. They come in a variety of sizes, and you can buy a bucket of them for about $1!

Real **freshwater**, or **natural**, pearls start at about 50 cents apiece, so use them sparingly — as a special accent bead, for example. In addition to their natural ivory color, they come in wonderful shades of pale pink, gold, purple, and shiny black.

* *See Techniques, pages 53–55.*

Swinging Hair Dangle

Swing some beads right along with your long hair or ponytail. Try a mix of stars and hearts — and don't forget a few crystals for some flash!

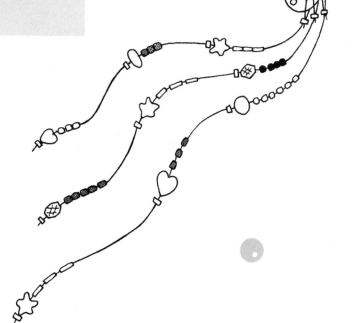

How difficult?
Easy!

Time:
15 minutes

What you need

10" (25 cm), 11" (27.5 cm), and 12" (30 cm) of 4-lb (1.85-kg) clear monofilament

Crimps (12 to 15)

Accent beads (12 to 16)

Bright, glittery seed beads and bugle beads (45 to 75)

Ruler or measuring tape

Tension clip

Needle-nose pliers

Glue

1 Attach a crimp* at one end of each monofilament strand. Slide on a shiny star or other accent bead and several seed beads or bugle beads.

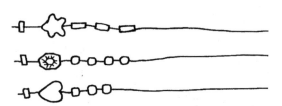

*See Techniques, pages 53–55.

2 Attach a crimp 3" to 4" (7.5 to 10 cm) up from the end. Add another accent bead and several seed beads or bugle beads. Follow that pattern to fill the strand. Repeat for the other two strands.

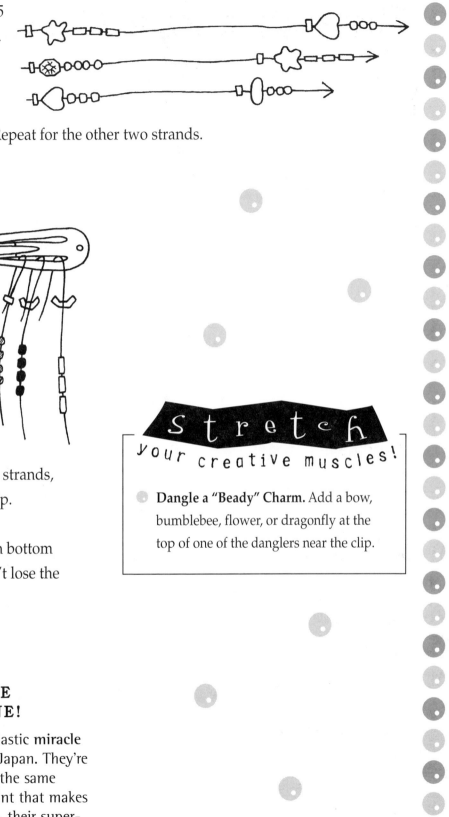

3 Slide a crimp onto the end of the monofilament. Loop the strand over the outside of the clip and back through the crimp; attach the crimp. Repeat with the other two strands, spacing them along the clip.

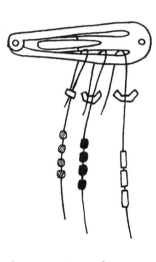

Add a drop of glue at each bottom crimp (to be sure you don't lose the beads) and let it dry.

Stretch your creative muscles!

● **Dangle a "Beady" Charm.** Add a bow, bumblebee, flower, or dragonfly at the top of one of the danglers near the clip.

The Savvy Bead Buyer

OUTSHINE EVERYONE!

Check out plastic **miracle beads** from Japan. They're coated with the same reflective paint that makes cars gleam — their super-bright colors are awesome!

Crystal & Pearl Cluster Illusion Headband

This circle of real pearls (see page 39) and crystals lies in a magical sparkling arc on your hair!

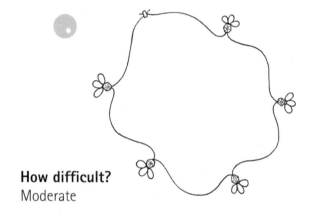

How difficult?
Moderate

Time:
1 hour

What you need

Foam board or paper

Pencil

Ruler or measuring tape

Beading needle

24" (60 cm) thin stretchy clear monofilament

4-mm crystals (5)

Teardrop-shaped 6-mm natural pearls (15)

Crimp

Needle-nose pliers

Scissors

1 Draw a line 3" (7.5 cm) line on the foam board or the paper.

2 Thread the needle with the monofilament. String one crystal and three pearls to the center. Bring the strand back through the crystal, forming a cluster of pearls.

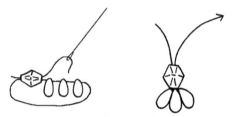

3 Using your line as a reference, form four more clusters, spacing them as shown:

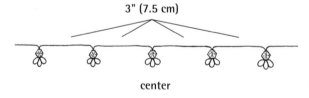

3" (7.5 cm)

center

4 Slip both ends of the monofilament through the crimp. Adjust the size of the headband to your head and attach the crimp*. Trim the ends.

*See Techniques, pages 53–55.

Magic Hair Sparkler

See if your friends can figure out what's holding this swinging sparkler in your hair! Buy the flat jewels in bags of mixed colors so you can make one to match every outfit.

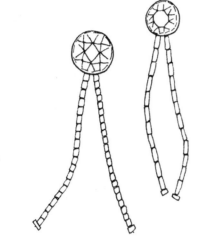

How difficult?
Easy!

Time:
20 minutes

What you need

8" (20 cm) of beading thread

Beading needle

Crimps (2)

Needle-nose pliers

Ruler or measuring tape

Sparkling, shiny bugle beads (enough to fill a 4"/10 cm strand), assorted colors

Adhesive-backed Velcro strip

½" (1 cm) flat, fake jewel, in a color that contrasts with your hair

Pencil or pen

Scissors

1 Thread the needle; attach a crimp* to the other end. String about 2" (5 cm) of beads.

2 Place the separated Velcro "hooked" side down. Put the jewel on the strip and trace around it. Cut out the shape and peel off the backing.

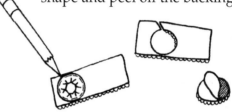

3 "Sandwich" the thread as shown between the adhesive side of the Velcro cutout and the jewel and press firmly.

4 String another 2" (5 cm) of beads. Attach a crimp on each thread to hold the beads firmly against the jewel. Trim the end of the thread.

See Techniques, pages 53–55.

Triple-Strand Illusion Headband

With this headband, nothing has to match if you don't want it to – it's a collection of your favorite beads, scattered wherever you like! Try a combination of glass seed beads and accent beads in colors that will contrast nicely with your hair.

How difficult?
Moderate

Time:
1 hour

What you need

24" (60 cm) of thick stretchy clear mono-filament (3)

Ruler or measuring tape

Pencil

Size 6 glass beads (70 to 90), in assorted colors and shapes

Accent beads (24 to 36)

Small crimps (21)

Needle-nose pliers

Large crimps

Scissors

Before you start:

You want the scattered beads to lie on the middle 7" to 8" (17.5 to 20 cm) of the strands. Fold each strand in half and follow the illustration. You'll attach your bead clusters between the crimp and the pencil mark.

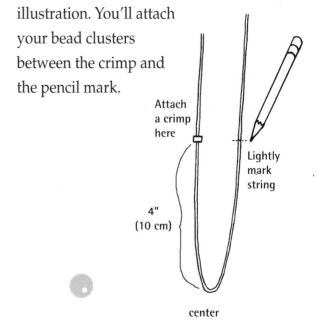

Attach a crimp here

Lightly mark string

4" (10 cm)

center

To make each strand:

1 Starting in the middle and working from one side to the other, attach a crimp*, slide on two to three glass beads and one to two accent beads, and attach another crimp.

Leave 1" to 2" (2.5 to 5 cm) between the crimps so that the beads can slide around. Continue until you've used all your beads.

To finish the headband:

2 Slide one large crimp over both ends of all three strands (six strands in all). Try the headbands on and adjust them to get the right length. Attach the crimp.

*See Techniques, pages 53–55.

*See Techniques, pages 53–55.

Quick Starts Tips!™

Crimp Won't Fit?

If you have trouble finding a crimp large enough for all three strands, use three large crimps to crimp the ends of each strand separately. Then, wear all three strands together.

PLAY WITH YOUR BEADS!

This illusion headband is the perfect way to combine odds and ends, like those leftover single beads or interesting accent beads. Mix sizes, make your patterns symmetrical, or scatter your beads unevenly — remember, you're the designer!

Not sure how to get started? Pin a piece of paper to your foam board and draw a line for each strand of your headband. Pin on different arrangements of beads until you have one you like. Then, tape your monofilament right below the line and transfer the beads, following your pattern.

Stretchy Rhinestone Illusion Headband

Suspend tiny sparks of light across your hair with this simple headband – the look is amazing!

How difficult?
Moderate

Time:
20 minutes

What you need

Pencil

Piece of foam board or paper

Ruler or measuring tape

16" (40 cm) of thin stretchy clear monofilament

Pronged rhinestone backs (3 or more)

30-mm flat, faceted rhinestones (3 or more)

Needle-nose pliers

Crimp

Scissors

1 Draw a line the length of your mono-filament on the foam board or paper. Use your ruler or measuring tape to mark it as shown.

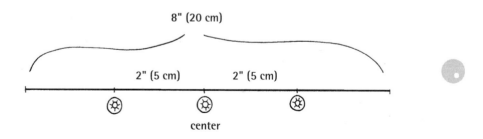

2 Lay the monofilament along your line. At the center, slip a pronged back under the monofilament.

Place one rhinestone into the backing. Press the prongs down with your fingers until the monofilament is held in place; then, tighten with pliers.

Be careful not to tighten too firmly, or the back will cut the monofilament. Repeat to add the remaining rhinestones.

3 Slide the ends of the monofilament through the crimp. Now, experiment with the length. Be sure the headband stretches easily on your head. When you have the length you want, attach the crimp*. Trim the ends of the monofilament if necessary.

Quick Starts Tips!™

Dangling Rhinestones

You want these rhinestones to lie on your hair correctly without flipping up. So, the headband should fit closely, but not too tightly around your head, and be sure to position the monofilament against the prongs as shown in step 2.

*See Techniques, pages 53–55.

Hair Snappers

Now here's the ultimate illusion of jewels afloat in your hair! Velcro is easier to attach (see page 43), but the snaps stay put, so there's no need to worry when the dancing gets wild!

How difficult?
Very easy!

Time:
1 minute per snapper to assemble (glue needs to cure overnight)

What you need

Large snaps

Waxed paper

Decorative items to attach to your snaps: flat jewels, pearl clusters, large accent beads

Strong glue*

Tweezers

Note: You'll need an adult's help to use this type of glue; please see page 58 before starting.

1 Separate the snaps; lay the tops prong side down on the waxed paper (that part is important!).

2 Being careful to keep the glue off your skin, squeeze a drop onto the flat side of the snap top as shown. Add the decoration on top and press together with tweezers. Let it dry overnight.

3 To wear, close the snap with a lock of hair between the two halves.

Stretch *your creative muscles!*

In Full Bloom! Glue on tiny fabric rosebuds or daisies for a garden in your hair!

Bold Barrettes

Women have been adorning their hair since time began, so why should things be any different today? With these playful barrettes, you can put a modern twist on an old custom. Instead of using shells and ivory beads, as our ancestors did, you can create jazzy, modern designs out of bugle beads and homemade clays in a variety of colors and styles!

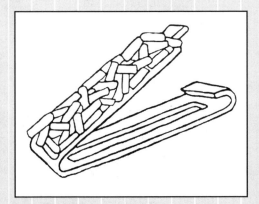

Bugle Bead Barrette

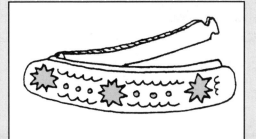

Colorful Clay Clasp

Bugle Bead Barrette

This craft is so easy to make that you'll want to wear it right away. The hardest part will be not touching it as it dries overnight!

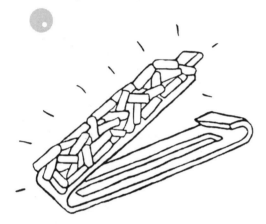

How difficult?
Easy!

Time:
10 minutes (overnight to dry)

What you need

Large sheet of paper

Bugle beads, color(s) of your choice

Metal barrette

Glue

1 Spread your bugle beads onto a sheet of paper. The beads should touch, but not overlap.

2 Spread the glue onto the side of the barrette that will be showing once it is clipped in your hair. Make sure that the entire surface is covered with glue.

3 Lay the barrette glue side down onto the bugle beads. Don't worry if there's too much glue. The white color will disappear as the glue dries.

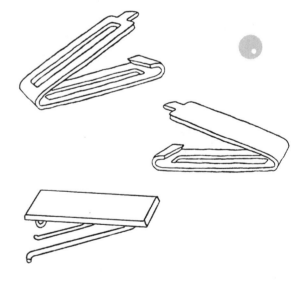

4 Place the barrette on a shelf to dry overnight.

Colorful Clay Clasp

These simple and very special barrettes can be made from leftover clay scraps. You can use polymer clays such as Sculpey and Fimo (be sure to follow the instructions on the package), or you can try some of my clay recipes (see page 52) for a truly customized design!

1 Cut or roll the clay into rectangular pieces slightly larger than the top of the barrette.

2 Using the toothpick or imprinting tools, carve or stamp a decorative design into the clay.

3 Place the decorated clay on the top of the barrette to dry so that the clay dries in the same curve as the barrette. Then, glue to the barrette top.

How difficult?
Easy!

Time:
20 minutes (overnight to dry)

What you need

Clay scraps

Toothpick

Imprinting materials such as nuts, macaroni, small rubber stamps, or buttons

Large, round container or shape

Metal barrette

Glue

stretch your creative muscles!

● **Name Your Clay.** Why not paint your name on your barrette with tempera paints, or carve the name first with a toothpick and then paint it with a thin brush for some dimension? Make barrettes with all your friends' names to give as party favors or holiday gifts.

MAKE YOUR OWN!

Try these homemade, ready-to-use clays for your barrettes and beads. When making beads, make your shapes and then let them harden overnight with a toothpick stuck through the middle to create the hole for stringing.

Tea Leaf Clay

This great clay will give your barrettes and beads a natural stone appearance. Put aside 2 tablespoons (30 ml) of used tea leaves. (For a sweet-smelling variation, use dried, crumbled rose petals instead.) In a bowl, combine 4 tablespoons (50 ml) flour, 1 tablespoon (15 ml) salt, and 1 tablespoon (15 ml) water. Gradually add the tea leaves. Stop before the clay starts to break apart. Work the clay into a firm ball and knead until you have a smooth clay.

Sawdust Clay

This clay will add an interesting texture to your items. In a bowl, mix 2 cups (500 ml) sawdust with 1 cup (250 ml) wallpaper paste (available at home supply stores). Slowly add water until a thick clay forms.

Salt Clay

This clay is a cinch! In a bowl, mix 1½ cups (375 ml) salt, and 4 cups (1 L) flour. Then, gradually add 1½ cups (375 ml) water. Knead well, adding water when it gets too crumbly, until the dough forms a ball around the spoon.

Coffee Clay

This clay concoction will make your craft look as if if was made of natural stone. In a bowl, combine 1 cup (250 ml) flour, ½ cup (125 ml) salt, 1 cup (250 ml) used coffee grounds, and ½ cup (125 ml) leftover coffee. When the mixture begins to form a ball, knead on a floured surface until the clay is smooth.

Techniques

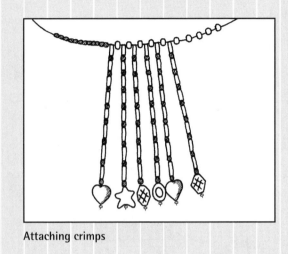
Attaching crimps

Here's a collection of handy how-to for accessory makers, from knots to kinks to crimps.

Tying Knots

A Single Knot

Left over right and through the loop.

Pull tight.

A Double Knot

Tie a single knot.

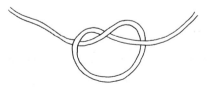

Now, go right over left and through the loop.

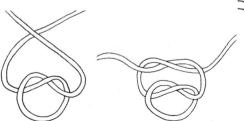

Pull tight.

A Lock Knot

A lock knot won't slip, whether you're tying elastic, thread, or monofilament!

Tying a lock knot with two ends:

Tie a single knot (see page 53). Then, bring the right end over and through the loop again.

Now, go right over left and through the loop. Then, pull tight.

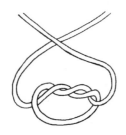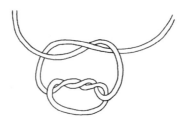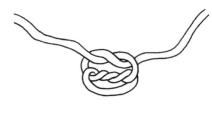

Tying a lock knot onto a loop:

Follow the steps shown above, using the loose end to go over or under the loop.

Forming a Kink

Use your needle-nose pliers to form a tiny loop to hold on your beads.

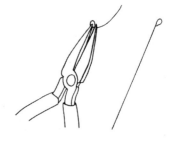

Attaching Jump Rings

Using your needle-nose pliers, open the jump ring by twisting it:

pull one end up
pull one end down

Avoid pulling the ends apart like this:

Attach your charm and then use the pliers to close the jump ring. Make sure the gap is tightly closed, especially if you're using very thin monofilament as your strand material.

Attaching Crimps

Positioning a Crimp

Slide the crimp over the strand material to the place where you want it.

Securing Your Beads

With needle-nose pliers, press the crimp shut, being careful not to cut through your strand.

Securing the Ends of a Strand

Slide the ends through the crimp from opposite sides.

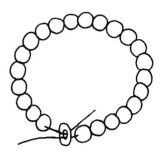

Close the crimp. If necessary, trim the ends so they're even.

"Must-Have" Supplies

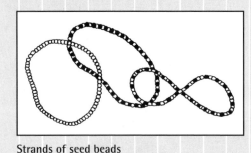

Strands of seed beads

One of the best things about making hairwear is that you don't need a lot of fancy tools and supplies. But as you get hooked on this hobby — and you will, trust me! — you'll quickly move on to more challenging pieces. Here's a run-down of the basics so that you'll know exactly what to look for in the store.

Beads, Beads, Beads: The Best Part of Hairwear

A bead is just about anything with a hole in it, and I can guarantee that you will never run out of beads to love. They come in an infinite variety of shapes, colors, materials, and sizes, from sparkly crystals and lustrous pearls, to shiny circles and tubes, to colorful flowers, butterflies, stars — you name it!

Accent Beads and Charms: These are special decorations that you use here and there for effect, rather than stringing an entire strand with them. You'll find them in glass, metal, plastic, wood, semiprecious stone, clay, and even tiny coils of colored wire. They're sold individually from bins in craft and bead shops, on small strands, or in packages of two or three.

Bugle Beads: Bugle beads are slender tubes of different lengths. Bugle beads have numbered sizes: the *longer* the bead, the *higher* the number.

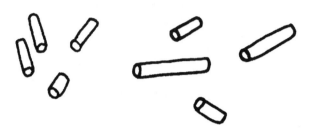

Quick Starts Tips!™

Bead Sizes

Even though beads from different countries will be labeled with the same number, they may be enough of a different size that they won't work with your other beads. When buying, use your eyes to make a good comparison.

Seed Beads: Small, donut-shaped spheres that resemble tiny seeds, these are the basic glass beads sold on strands, in tubes, or in small plastic bags.

The numbers indicate the size: the *higher* the number, the *smaller* the bead. Size 11's are the most common.

HOT ON THE TRAIL of the perfect bead!

Sometimes there are beads that nobody loves anymore — until you come along! You'll find them on jewelry at thrift shops, flea markets, garage sales, in your mom's and aunts' drawers, attics, and basements — perhaps even in your own jewelry box. These beads are ripe for cutting and restringing. Just be sure to ask first, so you don't cut up any jewelry that has special memories.

Handy Tools and Supplies

Your family probably already has most of the tools you'll need, and if not, none are expensive to buy.

Beading Needles

These long pieces of hair-thin wire are very flexible. Look for ones that have a large eye at the end so you can thread them easily (the eye will flatten to go through the littlest seed bead).

Wire needles don't last; they twist out of shape, so buy them by the pack and expect to go through a lot.

Foam Board

A sheet of foam board, cut down to a comfortable size, makes a great work surface. You can stick quilting pins into it to hold your jewelry steady as you work and mark the board for spacing beads evenly.

Plus, if you have to put your project away for a while, the pins will hold your work-in-progress in place.

Glue

Occasionally, you'll need a little glue. Usually, it's just a drop to secure something — white craft glue will be fine. Some glues decay plastic, though (which includes monofilament), so check the label.

One project in this book requires a strong glue as noted. But the better a glue sticks, the more toxic it seems to be. When you use any glue that is not labeled "nontoxic," please ask an adult for help. It's very important to keep it off your skin and to avoid breathing it.

Measuring Tape

Use it to measure your stringing material and your hairwear for just the look you want!

Needle-Nose Pliers

Choose a pair that fits comfortably in your hand and look for the pointiest "nose" you can find.

Quilting Pins

These sewing pins (also called ball-point pins) have large heads, so it's easy to push and pull them in and out of your foam board.

Scissors or Nail Clippers

You can use either of these to cut most beading wire, but if you use them frequently, the blades will be ruined for cutting anything else. A sturdy pair of inexpensive kid's scissors is perfect.

Tweezers

Use them for picking up little things (like tiny beads) your fingers can't and for pressing wires tightly together.

Wire Cutters

You may want to use these to cut your beading wire.

Quick Starts Tips!™

Storing Your Supplies

So you can always find zx, keep your supplies and tools in little containers labeled "Findings," "Stringing Supplies," "Tools," etc. I like small, inexpensive plastic buckets from home supply stores; I can easily see what's inside, and they stack to fit on shelves. Recycled yogurt cartons, plastic food storage containers, and baskets will also do the job. Little glass bottles or jars and inexpensive plastic tackle boxes make great bead holders.

If you're careful with your tools, they'll last forever. I still have the needle-nose pliers I bought when I was 12 years old. When I'm finished, they go back in my bright red easy-to-find toolbox that I've loved for years.

Findings

Findings are all the little "nuts and bolts" that you use to hold your hairwear together. Take a quick look through your jewelry box — you already have most of these pieces on your existing jewelry; you just may not have known what they were called.

Crimps

These soft metal circles are first strung and then pressed flat with needle-nose pliers. Crimps are used to close loops of monofilament or wire (where knots wouldn't hold very well) and to hold beads in place.

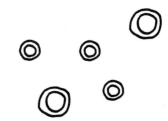

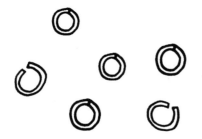

Jump Rings

Little circles of metal to attach to a charm.

Pronged Rhinestone Backs

This flat disk (measured in millimeters) holds a flat-backed rhinestone onto a strand of beads.

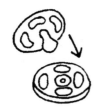

Snaps

These two-piece attachments, most often made of metal, can be found in sewing stores and notions departments. They come in various sizes, but the largest ones are the best for hairwear. One side has a prong protruding from the center, and the other side has a hole into which the prong is inserted.

Stringing Materials

Beading Thread

It pays to go for the good-quality stuff. It's durable and it won't fray. The last thing you want is for your strand to break!

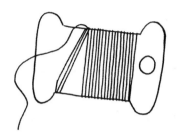

Beading Wire

A strong but flexible wire. The thickness is called the "gauge": the *higher* the number, the *thinner* the wire.

Elastic Thread

Stretchy sewing thread, available in different thicknesses.

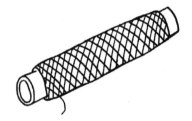

Monofilament

"Mono" is a strong, flexible nylon strand material used for bead stringing and illusion jewelry. It is also called "illusion cord."

Regular monofilament is sold in different sizes by weight: the *higher* the number of pounds, the *stronger* the stuff.

The stretchy version (sometimes sold as "clear stretchy string,") comes in thick and thin.

Hair Holders

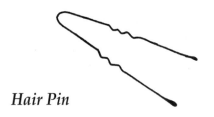

Hair Pin

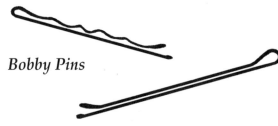

Bobby Pins

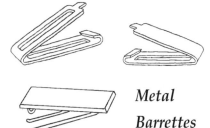

Metal Barrettes

Elastic Tieback

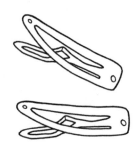

Tension Hair Clips

Plastic Combs

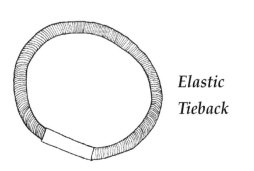

SAFETY CHECK!

If your household has small children, please don't leave your beading supplies and tools within their reach. This includes dropped beads — they might choke on them.

Be careful with your needles, especially near your eyes. Avoid letting needles roll onto the floor or into chairs — they're very hard to find.

Index

B
barrettes, 49–51
beads
    accent beads, 31, 44, 56
    bugle beads, 12, 14, 50, 57
    coil beads, 8
    crystal beads, 16, 17, 40
    fringe, beaded, 11–13
    iridescent beads, 20, 30
    making beads, 14, 133
    miracle beads, 41
    old beads, 57
    opalescent beads, 20
    pearls (see pearls)
    seed beads, 20, 29, 57
    size, 12, 14, 29, 57
    sorting, 7, 29
    stringing techniques, 27, 28–29
bugle beads, 12, 14, 50, 57
butterfly hairwear, 37

C
coil beads, 8
combs, 19, 62
crimps
    attaching, 55
    with beaded fringe, 13
    combining strands, 45

D
double-weaving, 28–29
dragonfly "beady," 20–21

E
elastic, 61

F
findings, 60. (See also crimps; jump
    rings; snaps)
fishing line, 36
flower hairwear, 18, 19
foam board, 45, 58
fringe, beaded, 11–13

G
glue, 58

I
illusion hairwear, 35–48
    designing, 36, 45

J
jump rings, 22, 34, 55, 60

K
kinks
    avoiding in strand material, 36
    forming to secure beads, 54
knots, 53–54

L
ladybug "beady," 34
lock knot, 54

M
measuring tape, 58
miracle beads, 41
monofilament, 36, 61. (See also
    fishing line)

N
nail clippers, 59
needle-nose pliers, 58
needles for beading, 58, 62

O
old beads, 57

P
pearls
    freshwater vs. faux (pretend), 39
    in hair accessories, 18, 38, 42

Q
quilting pins, 59

R
rhinestones, 47
    pronged rhinestone backs, 60

S
safety tips, 62
scissors, 59
seed beads. (See also beads)
    defined, 57
    finishes, 20
    holes, 27, 29
    size and shape, 20, 29, 57
snaps, 60
star hairwear, 25–27

strands
    multiple strands, 8, 44
    single strands, 5
stringing techniques, 27, 28–29
supplies for making hairwear, 56–58
    beads, 56–57 (see also beads)
    findings, 60
    storing supplies, 59, 62
    stringing materials, 61 (see also
        thread; wire)
    tools, 58–59

T
T-shirts, 24, 27
techniques, 53–55
    attaching "beady" charms, 22
    attaching jump rings, 60
    crimping, 55
    double-weaving, 28–29
    fringing, 13
    illusion technique, 36
    kinking to secure beads, 55
    rhinestone techniques, 47
    tying knots, 53–54
thread,
    elastic, 61
    fishing line, 36
    in double-weaving, 33
    knotting techniques, 53–54
    monofilament, 35, 36, 61
    vs. wire, 33 (see also wire)
tools for making hairwear, 58–59
tweezers, 59

W
wire
    cutting, 59
    kinks, forming, 55
    thickness (gauge), 61
    vs. thread, 33, (see also thread)